Published by Storycomic LLC
info@storycomic.com

Printed in the United States

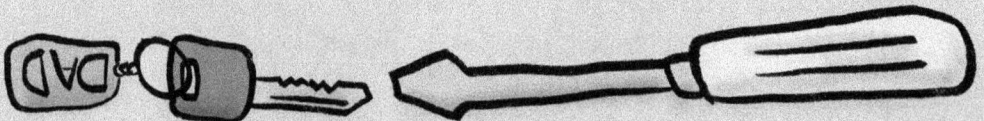

For Mr.Richards:

My Highschool School
English teacher who first
taught me that it is okay to
make a fool of oneself to
lift the spirts of others.

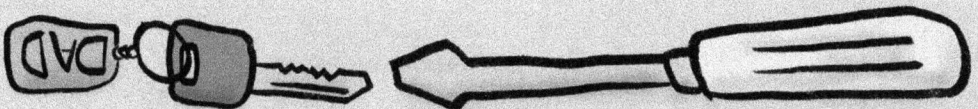

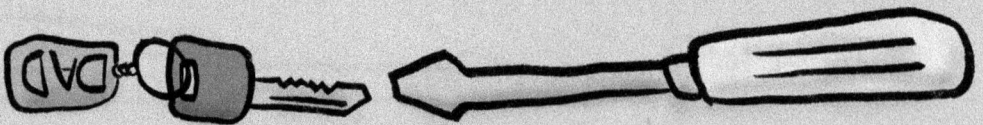

CONTENTS

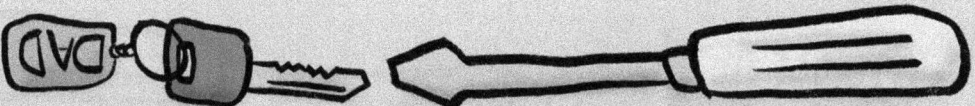

Written, compiled, edited, designed, watered, fed, washed, and illustrated

by:

Barney Smith at storycomic.com

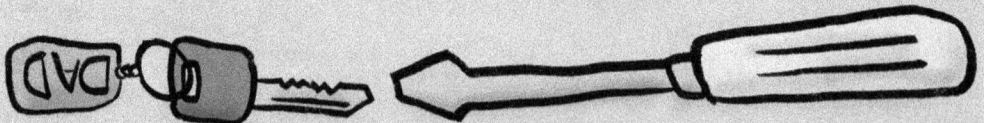

INTRODUCTION

Laughter is a magical thing. It has the power to break down barriers, connect people, and brighten even the darkest of days. And that's exactly what we set out to do with our first book of jokes. In the midst of a challenging year, we made the conscious effort to spread some joy and happiness by sharing a daily dad joke online.

At first, it was just a small gesture, a way to bring a smile to the faces of our friends and followers. But as we continued to share our silly puns and clever one-liners, we realized that something special was happening. People from all walks of life were coming together, united by a shared love of laughter and connection.

We received messages of gratitude from all corners of the world, thanking us for bringing some light and positivity into their lives. And it was then that we knew we had to keep going. We had to keep sharing our jokes, keep spreading the love, and keep reminding ourselves and others that even in the darkest of times, there is always something to smile about.

And so, we're back with a sequel, filled with even more jokes and puns to bring a little bit of warmth and inspiration into your day. We invite you to join us on this journey of laughter and connection, as we celebrate the power of humor to uplift and inspire. Because at the end of the day, it's the small things that can make the biggest difference in our lives, and a good joke is sometimes all it takes to bring a little bit of light into the world.

-Barney Smith

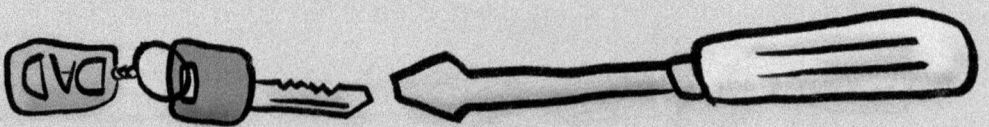

CHAPTER 1:

CUSTODIAL

QUIPS

Two buckets were in a bar. One
bucket says, "Are you feeling sick,
friend?"
"No, why?"
"You are a little pail."

A B-flat, a E-flat and a G-flat walk
into a bar.
The bartender says, "Sorry I don't
serve minors".

Why did the cookie cry?
Because his mother was a
wafer so long .

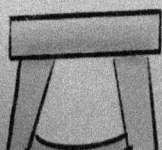

Space heaters are the perfect
housewarming gifts.

I asked my wife why we never talk
about gravity.
She said it just never seems to
come up.

What do you call an apology
written in dots and dashes?
Re-Morse code.

I threw a boomerang a couple
years ago;
I now live in constant fear.

A bird with no beak was
born to succeed.

What do you call a nun who just
passed her bar exam?
A Sister-In-Law

It's good to know that a drawer put in
backwards is a reward.

Doctor: "Sir, I'm afraid
your DNA is backwards."
Me: "And?"

I have an irrational fear of
over-designed buildings.
It's a complex complex
complex.

My friend told me that he failed his exam in Aboriginal Music.
I asked him, "Did ya redo it?"

Why do they call the season autumn ?
Because autumn leaves fall off the trees

If you spell wrong, wrong, you haven't spelled it right, therefore it's wrong. But it is also not wrong, because it's not right.

Dear Autocorrect,
I am getting tired
of your shirt!

I have been trying to understand why my candle has such bad insomnia.
I guess there is no rest for the wicked.

Spaces between ladder rungs have increased because people are getting taller.
Manufacturers claim it is due to climb it change.

I've been thinking about taking up meditation. I figure it's better than
sitting around doing nothing.

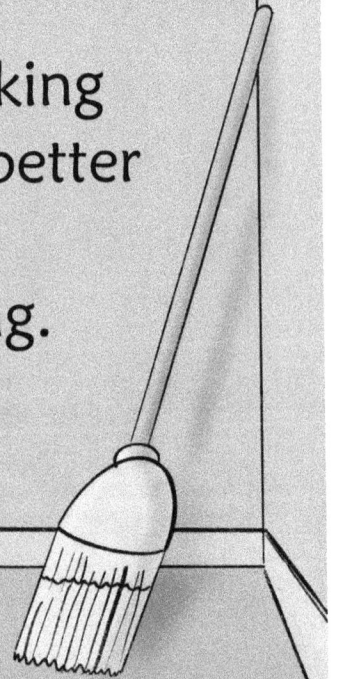

I was walking through a quarry..I said
to the foreman," that sure is a big
rock!"
"Boulder", he corrected me. So I
stuck out my chest and shouted
"THAT SURE IS A BIG ROCK!!"

I never trusted lizards...
right from the gecko

If you wear cowboy clothes,
are you in ranch dressing?

I know this great joke about
flying lizards,
but it tends to drag on.

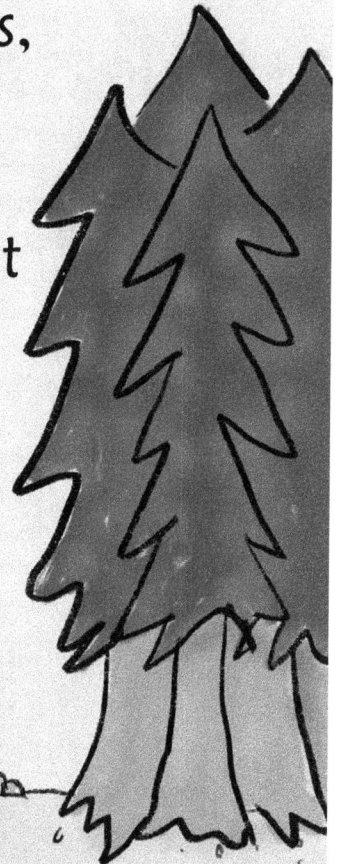

How did Bilbo survive the entire
Lord of the Rings trilogy?
Because old Hobbits die hard...

I just read 3 pages of the dictionary
and learned Next to Nothing.

Learning English is difficult, but it can
be taught through tough thorough
thought though.

What do scholars eat when they're
hungry?
Academia nuts.

I hate perforated lines.
They are tearable.

Someone has glued my pack
of cards together.
I don't know how to deal with it

I was playing Bonopoly last night.
It's the same as Monopoly except
the streets have no name.

What do you call a caveman
who is walking slowly?
A Meanderthal.

I put a dart board on the ceiling.
It made me throw up.

What kind of pizza do
pilots prefer?
Plain.

I changed my password to "incorrect". So, whenever I forget what it is the computer will say "Your password is incorrect".

For the 10th year in a row, my coworkers voted me "the most secretive guy" in the office.
I can't tell you how much this award means to me.

Why shouldn't you write with a broken pencil?
Because it's pointless.

Not all math jokes are terrible, only sum.

What crime do blacksmiths most commonly get charged with?
Forgery.

A genie granted me one wish, so I said "I just want to be happy."
Now I'm living in a cottage with 6 dwarves and working in a mine.

How many meteorologists does it take to change a light bulb?
Today, there's a 70% chance of one.

My friend wishes to become an archaeologist.
I am worried his life will be in ruins.

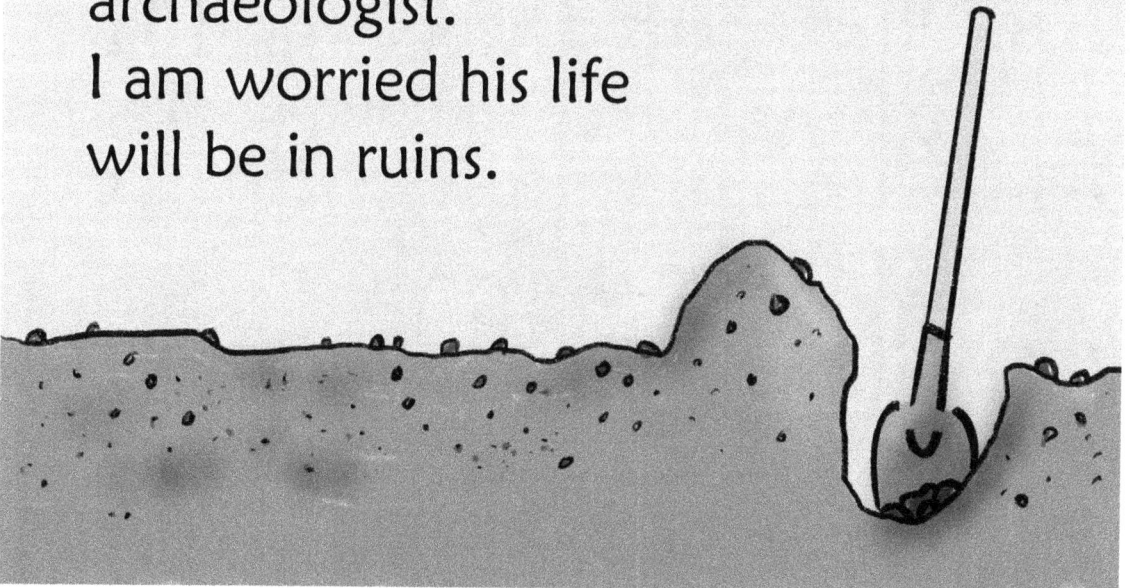

I asked my dad how he felt about having the best son in the world.
He told me to ask my grandpa.

I asked my wife if I was the first one to kiss her.
She replied yes, the others were nines and tens.

What smells the best at a Thanksgiving dinner?
Your nose.

If I had a nickel for every bread pun, I would have a pun per nickel.

Why do clumsy farmers make good DJs?
They're always dropping the beets.

I hate it when I think I'm buying ORGANIC vegetables, but when I come home I realize they're just REGULAR doughnuts.

Why did the cowboy have a weiner dog? Somebody told him to get a long little doggy.

How does a train hear another train coming?
With its engineers.

When I lived on a houseboat, I started dating the girl next door. Eventually we just drifted apart.

Why do seagulls fly over the sea? Because if they flew over the bay, they'd be bagels.

I hear they are developing a mind controlled air freshener.
It makes scents when you think about it.

What do you call two octopuses that look the same?
Itenticle.

What do you call a priest who
becomes a lawyer?
A father-in-law.

When I moved into my new igloo
my friends threw me a surprise
house warming party.
Now I'm homeless.

So far Humpty Dumpty is having a
terrible winter... It's a shame because
he had such a great fall!

I used to be poor. Then I bought a
thesaurus, and now I'm impecunious.

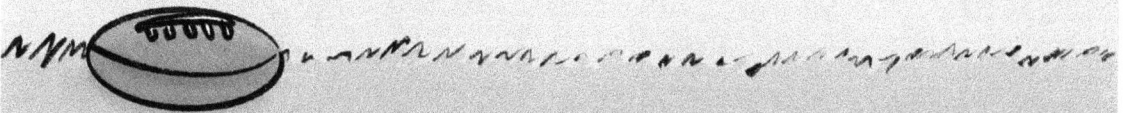

You know, people say they pick
their nose, but I feel like I was
just born with mine.

If you think that your microwave
collecting data and the TV
spying on you is bad enough,
the vacuum cleaner has
been gathering dirt on
you for years.

I was raised by a pack of
wild hyenas, life was tough
and food was scarce, but
boy did we laugh.

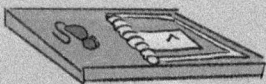

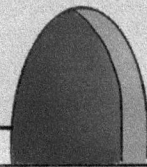

Don't you really hate people when they use really big words to make themselves look perspicacious

Did you hear about the cat who ate a ball of yarn?
She had mittens.

Muffins spelled backwards is what you do when you take them out of the oven.

If you didn't properly make tea, would you get a steep fine?

3 hardest things for a man to say:
1: I was wrong
2: I need help
3: Worcestershire Sauce

I've been planning on doing
something spontaneous for a while
now.

I was in a taxi the other day
and the driver said 'do you
mind if I put some music on?'
I said 'Not at all'
He said 'Kiss?'
I said 'Let's listen to the
music first and see
how we feel'

My neighbors listen to great music.
Whether they like it or not.

Today I saw an ad that said, "radio
for sale, $1, volume stuck on full."
I thought, "I can't turn that down."

Apparently the song "Jenny" from
Tommy Tutone has been played by
radio stations all over the world
8,675,309 times.

Accordion to a recent study,
7 out of 10 people do not
notice when a word
in a sentence is
replaced by a musical
instrument.

We Wi. R zdX

I bought a house with a 4 foot
high ceiling.
I can't stand living there.

What is the scariest tree?
BamBOO!

One chickpea said to another "You
don't look too good". The other
replied "I know, I falafel".

My wife said I should do lunges to
stay in shape.
That would be a big
step forward.

What do you do if you see a fireman?
Put it out, man.

In other news... a local art gallery
find themselves in dire straits.
Apparently they sold their Monet for
nothing.

Doctor: Relax, David. It's just a small
surgery, don't panic.
Me: But my name isn't David.
Doctor: I know. I'm David.

Did you hear about the population
of Ireland?
It's Dublin.

What did the cupcake tell its frosting?
"I'd be muffin without you."

Just picked up a Humpty Dumpty toy from Aldi. It's brilliant, It came with Aldi King's horses and Aldi King's men.

What's Harry Potter's favorite way to get down a hill?
Walking...JK, Rowling.

Saw a squirrel that couldn't make up his mind today.
He was on the fence all day.

What does a house wear?
Address.

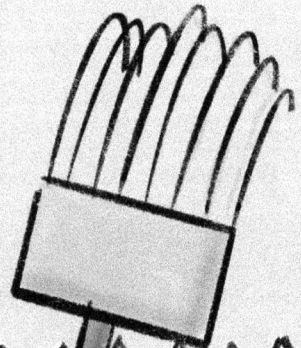

I don't wear mittens everyday. I guess you could say I wear them intermittenly.

I can't remember what 51, 6, and 500 are in Roman Numerals.
I'm LIVID.

What do I know about Bonsai trees?
Very little...

Do you know what
makes me smile?
Face muscles

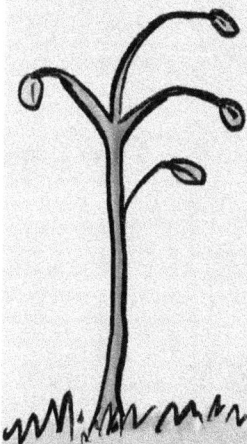

Did you hear about the mathematician who was afraid of negative numbers?
He would stop at nothing to avoid them.

I'm not saying your house is haunted, but I think a ghost just ate all of your Gummy Bears while you were in the bathroom.

Someone asked me what the 9th letter of the alphabet was.
It was a complete guess but I was right.

What does the dentist of the year get?
A little plaque.

I've been trying to come up with a joke about momentum, but I just can't seem to get it going.

I invented a car that moves only when the driver is silent.
It goes without saying.

Cosmetics jokes are really difficult to make-up.

What did the two pieces of bread
say on their wedding day?
It was loaf at first sight.

I started to count my tools at 10pm
But I stopped after the seventh
because it was tool eight.

I dressed up as a screwdriver
this past Halloween.
It wasn't the best
costume, but I
still turned a lot
of heads.

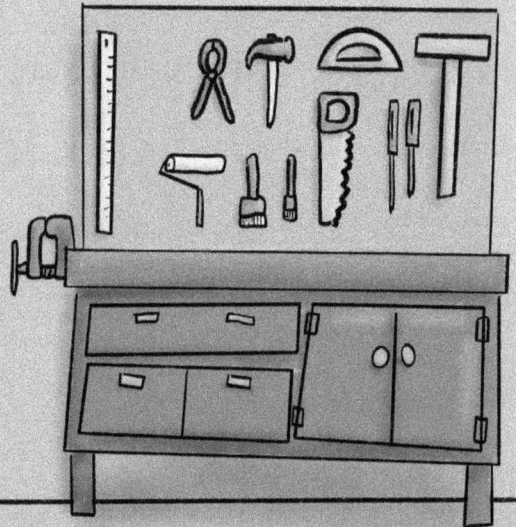

At the bar last night, a guy got his ear pierced right in front of me. On a related note, I really suck at darts.

My wife gets annoyed if I mess with her red wine, so I've added fruit and lemonade to it and now she's sangria than ever.

Muhammad Ali walked into a bar, ordered a drink and proceeded to pay with ceramic money.
The bartender responded
"I can't accept this.
Your cash is clay."

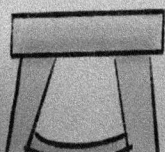

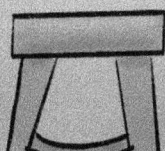

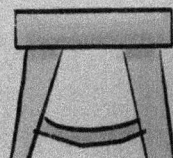

I quit my job making unscented deodorant.
I've had enough of that non-scents.

What keeps tree limbs from falling?
Their stickiness,

What did the grape do when he got stepped on?
He let out a little wine.

There is now a 12-step program for compulsive talkers.
It's called On Anon Anon.

CHAPTER 2:
SIRE
SARCASMS

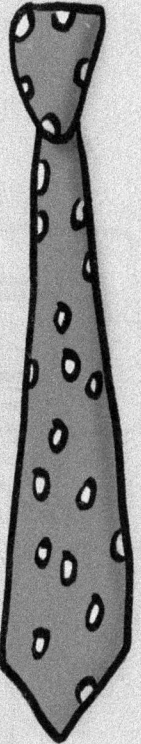
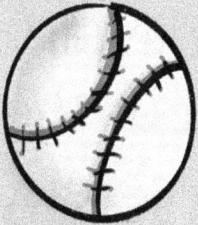

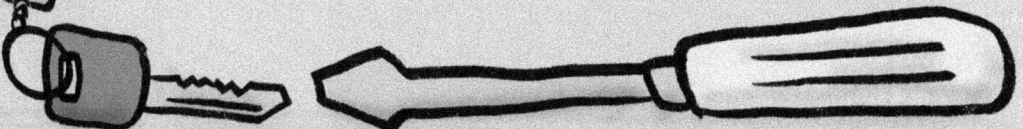

I accidentally sprayed deodorant in my mouth.
Now when I talk, I have this weird axe scent.

Tonight's clairvoyant meeting cancelled due to unforeseen circumstances.

How do you console an English teacher?
There, their, they're...

The decision to restrict waterfowl in the aviary was very difficult, but the zookeeper has no egrets.

There was the person who sent
ten puns to friends, with the
hope that at least one of the puns
would make them laugh.
No pun in ten did

The scarecrow said,
"This job isn't for everyone,
but hay, it's in my jeans."

Not all construction work is
equally enjoyable.
For example, enlarging a drilled
hole is boring, but fastening
pieces of metal together
is riveting.

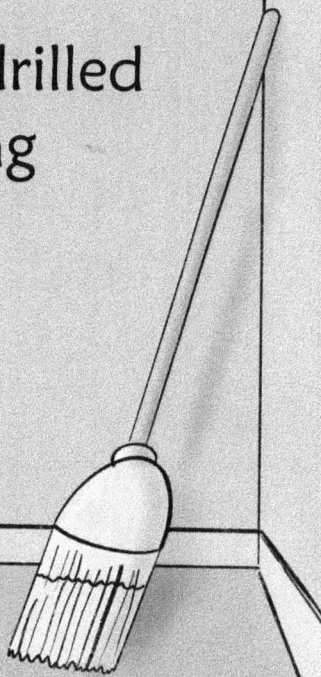

I told my wife I wanted to be
cremated.
She made an appointment
for Tuesday.

Me: Waiter, this soup is cold.
Waiter: It's Gazpacho.
Me: Gazpacho, this soup is cold.

I regret buying that straitjacket now.
I thought it would look
good on me but I just
couldn't pull it off.

I got locked out of my
Italian restaurant.
Gnocchi.

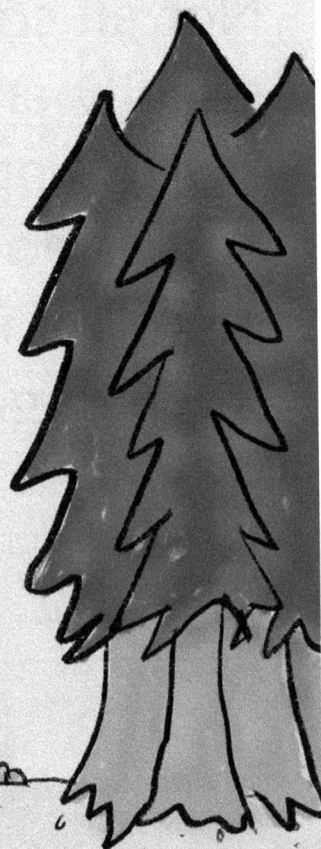

If a dentist pulls the wrong tooth, is it accidental?
I thought I saw an eye-doctor on an Alaskan island, but it turned out to be an optical Aleutian .

Without a doubt my favorite
Robin Williams movie is 'Mrs Fire'.

What do you get when you cross
a cow with an octopus?
A visit from the Ethics Committee
and immediate withdrawal
of your funding.

Irony is the opposite
of wrinkly.

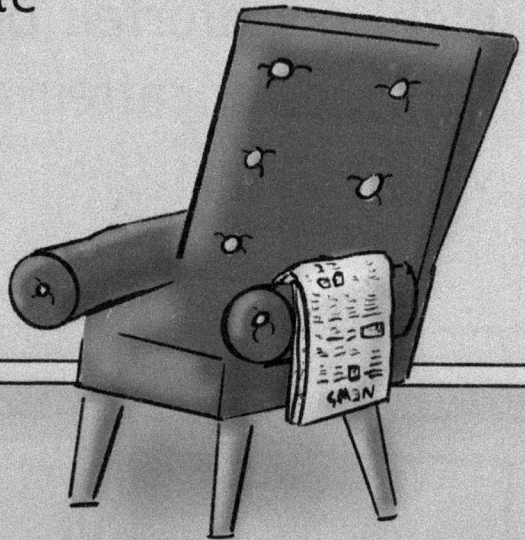

I struggle with Roman Numerals
until I get to 159.
Then it just CLIX.

I'm not so sure about this daylight
savings time thing...
I give it six months.

Going to the back of the boat
where you are not allowed to go
could get you a stern warning.

I Before E, except when your
foreign neighbor Keith receives
eight counterfeit beige sleighs
from feisty caffeinated
weightlifters.

What does "idk" stand for?
I've asked lots of people, but
nobody seems to know.

A and C were going to prank
their friend...
But they just letter B

While filling out a job application,
they had a section for "previous
life experience", so I wrote down
that I was a Pharaoh in 2300 B.C.

How do you know
when you run out
of invisible ink?

How does music say goodbye?
Audios!

What do you get when you cross a
snail with a porcupine?
A slowpoke

A guy walks into a bar...
and was immediately disqualified
from the limbo contest.

Nothing is built in the USA anymore.
I just bought a TV. It said, "Built in
Antenna". I don't even know
where that is!

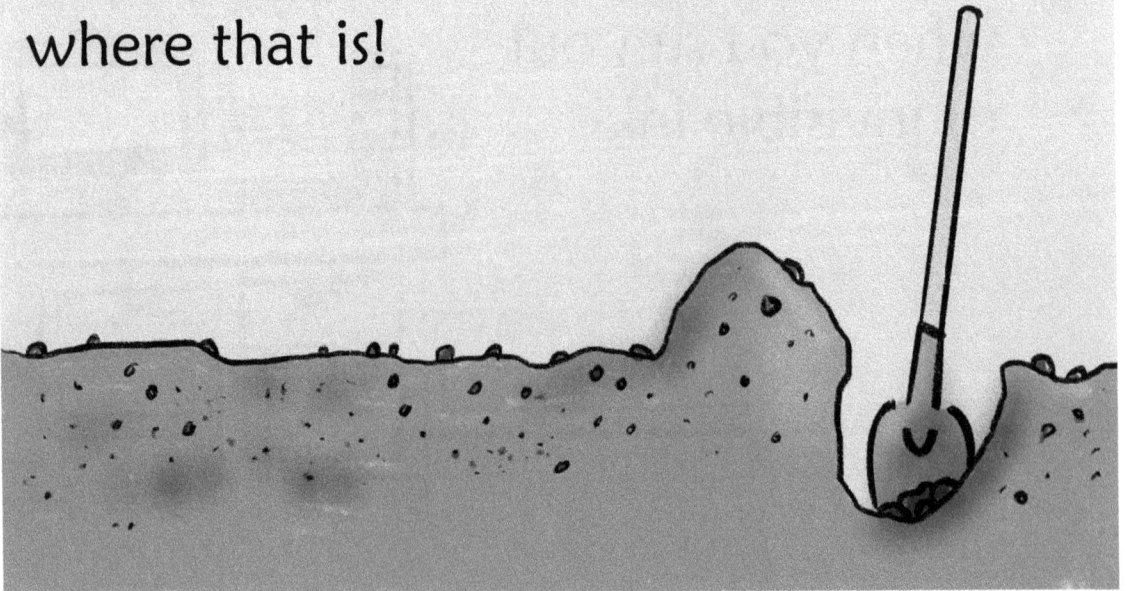

Where do animals go when their tails fall off?
The retail store.

My wife has asked me to stop making police related puns.
I said, "OK. I'll give it arrest.

What do you call two monkeys who share an Amazon account?
Prime mates.

My wife and I had this long argument as to which vowel is the most important.
I won.

37

The internet connection at my farm was really poor, so I moved the modem to the barn.
Now I have a stable WiFi.

I suffer from a compulsion to touch dairy products.
I'm feeling much butter now.

Where do sheep get their hair cut?
At the baa baas.

A farmer had 297 cows. When he rounded them up, he had 300

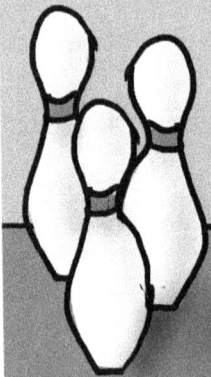

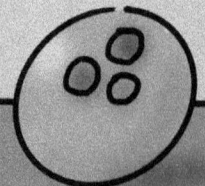

I thought I saw a sausage fly past the window, but it was a seabird. I think I've taken a tern for the wurst.

What do you call a group of killer whales playing instruments?
An Orca-stra.

Why aren't jet skis called boatercyles?

Surfing is a good choice for people who like skateboarding but wish it had more sharks.

Is it okay to listen to AM radio in the afternoon?

Me: I'm not saying a word without my lawyer present.
Cop: You ARE the lawyer.
Lawyer: So where's my present?

I used to play piano by ear.
Now I use my hands.

We all know where the Big Apple is but does anyone know where Minneapolis?

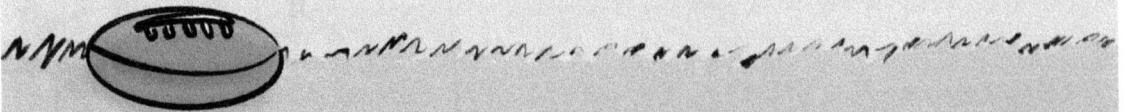

I can't believe someone broke into my house and stole all my fruit.
I am peachless !

The person who invented the Ferris Wheel never met the person who invented the Merry-Go-Round.
They traveled in different circles.

My twin brother called me from prison.
He said: "You know how we finish each other's sentences?"

Just so everybody's clear...
I'm going to put my glasses on.

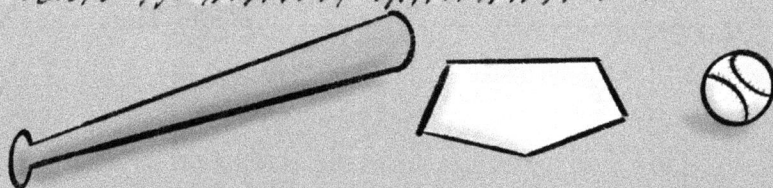

How do you get two whales
in a car?
Start in England and drive West.

I learned 2 important lessons today.
I can't remember the first lesson,
but the second one is I have to start
writing things down.

On average people use 3 covers
when they sleep at night.
This is just a blanket statement.

Why do they call it a pretzel?
Because it's knot bread.

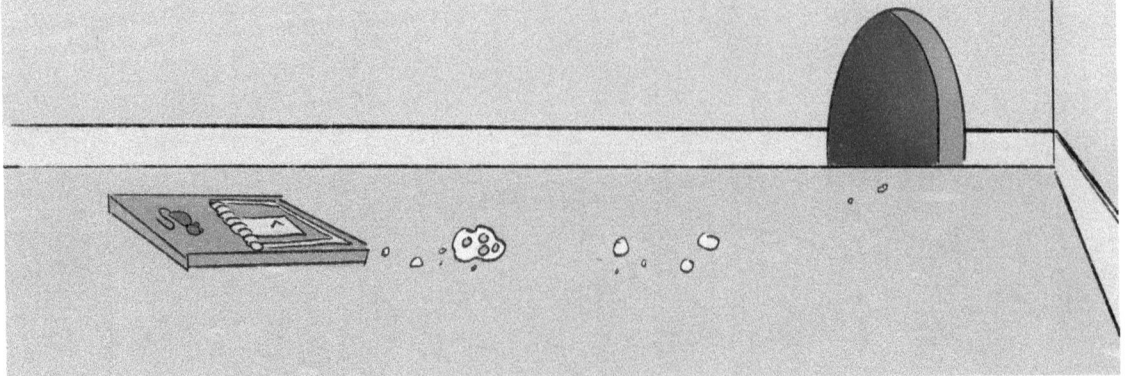

What does the Easter Bunny get for making a basket?
Two points, just like anyone else.

"I once played golf with the actors from The A-Team but we only managed 17 holes."
"Missed a tee?"
"Yeah, he was there of course."

At a job interview I filled my glass of water until it overflowed a little.
"Nervous?" asked the interviewer.
"No. I always give 110%".

My wife thinks it's weird that I stare
at the window during a heavy
rainstorm.
It would be a lot less weird if
she would just let me in.

I ordered some German food over
the Internet.
The sauerkraut has arrived but the
wurst has yet to come.

I gave my friend a peach.
He said, "Thanks, but I would rather
have a pear."
So I gave him
another peach.

My boss asked me why I only get sick on work days.
I said it must be my weekend immune system.

My 4-year-old daughter has been learning Spanish all year and she still can't say the word 'please'
Which I think is poor for four.

My dad was bragging about his new hearing aid. "State of the Art," he said, "It cost me a fortune."
I asked: "Awesome what type is it? "
He said: "Two thirty."

I think the woman at the airline's check-in just threatened me. She looked me and said, 'Window or aisle?'
I replied, 'Window or you'll what?'

I saw a microbiologist today.
He was much bigger than I expected.

Did you hear about the bankrupt poet who ode everyone?

When I was young, I was poor but after years of hard work, I am no longer young.

Finally, my winter fat has gone.
Now I have spring rolls.

What did Obi-Wan tell Luke
at the rodeo?
"Use the horse, Luke!"

Two cups of yogurt walk into a
country club.
"We don't serve your kind here."
"Why not?" one yogurt asks.
"We're cultured."

A shark can swim faster than me,
but I can run faster. So in a triathlon,
it would all come down to
who is the better cyclist.

Why should you never mention the number 288?
It's two gross.

I got trapped in a bidding war for a house, because my wife
loved the lengthy corridor.
Now I'm in it for the
long hall.

I checked my friend into a rehab center for his addiction to placebos.
Well, he thinks it's a rehab center...

What do you call a mother
who can't draw?
Tracy.

9 out of 10 people who are afraid of hurdles never get over it.

Optimist: The glass is 1/2 full.
Pessimist: The glass is 1/2 empty.
Excel: The glass is January 2nd.

Steps for surviving on a dessert island:
1. Check spelling.
2. If correct, enjoy.

Don't use double negatives.
They're a big no no.

If you are being chased by a pack of taxidermists, do not play dead.

I'm not saying I'm attractive, but when I take my clothes off in the bathroom.
I turn the shower on.

I'm under the weather today, also so is everyone else.
That's how weather works.

What do you call someone who studies dad jokes?
A sigh-entist.

I visited the birthplace of the man
who invented the toothbrush.
There's no plaque.

How do you fix a broken pizza?
With tomato paste.

Do mascara and lipstick ever argue?
Sure, but then they makeup.

Cookie dough is the
sushi of desserts.

I asked my friend to spell
'won ton' backwards.
He said "Not now."

I've forgotten all my boomerang jokes, but I'm sure they'll come back to me.

My uncle works for a company that makes bicycle wheels.
He's the Spokesman.

Bought a new muzzle for my pet duck the other day.
Nothing fancy, but it fits the bill.

My friend works at the police station drawing sketches of suspects.
She's a con artist.

A Polar Bear walks into a bar and says, "I'll have a gin and...... tonic." The Bartender asks, "Why the big pause?" The Polar Bear replies, "I don't know, I've always had them."

What did one nut say as he chased another nut? I'm a cashew!

What do you call a singing laptop? A Dell.

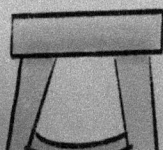 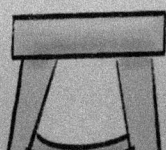 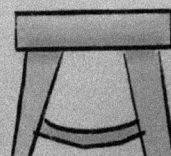

What's the difference between a witch and c-a-s-t-s ?
One casts spells and the other spells casts.

Me: What's the difference between an elephant and a matterbaby?
Wife: What's a matterbaby?
Me: Nothing, but thanks for asking.

What pronouns does chocolate use?
Her/she.

My wife got me a jar of dirt for my birthday.

Sundays are always a little sad, but the day before is a sadder day.

The great thing about stationery stores is they are always in the same place.

My cloning experiments finally paid off. I'm so excited, I'm beside myself.

I just found out Stefi Graff has a sister called Polly. I'm not even lying.

My dog used to chase people on a bike a lot.
It got so bad I had to take his bike away.

Without geometry life is pointless.

What did Friday say to Saturday and Sunday when they were about to give up?
"Weekend do it."

Why do cows have hooves and not feet?
They lactose.

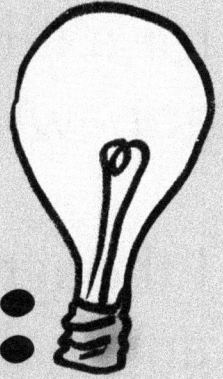

CHAPTER 3:

MENTOR MOCKERIES

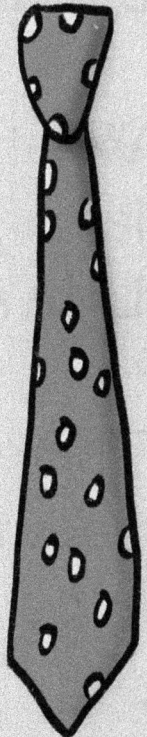

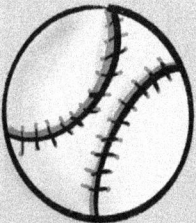

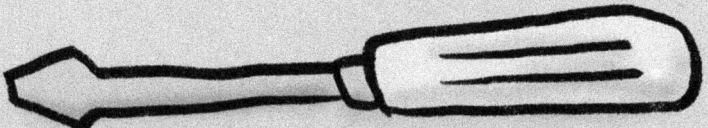

We got a new dog and I named
him 'Shark'
I took him to the beach, lost him
for a little while, and well, things
got awkward real fast.

I thought about going on
an all-almond diet,
but that's just nuts.

What do you call a laughing
jar of mayonnaise?
LMAYO.

There's a new theatre production
about a thesaurus.
It's a play on words.

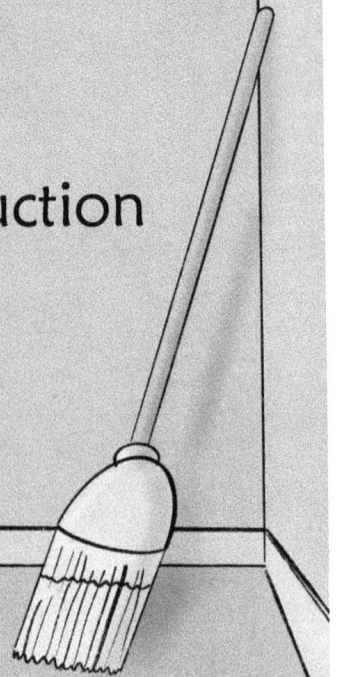

How do Ewoks communicate over long distances?
With Ewokie Talkies.

Guess who I bumped into on my way to get my glasses fixed?
Everybody.

I wear a stethoscope so that in a medical emergency I can teach people a valuable lesson about assumptions.

You know what they say about cliffhangers...

Where do young trees go to learn?
Elementree school.

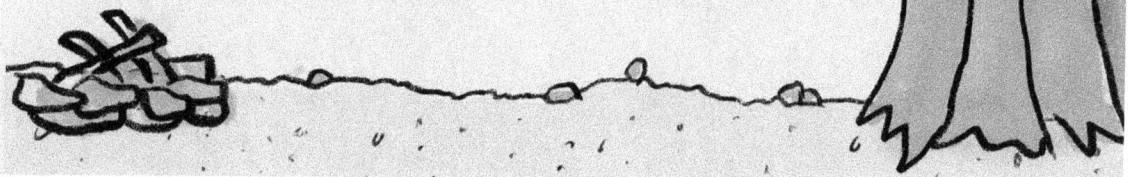

What do you get if you stand
between two llamas?
Llamanated.

We started a band and called it
"Books"
So no one can judge us by our
covers.

The salesman told me, "This sofa
will seat 5 people without any
problems."
I said, "Where the heck
am I going to find 5
people without
any problems?"

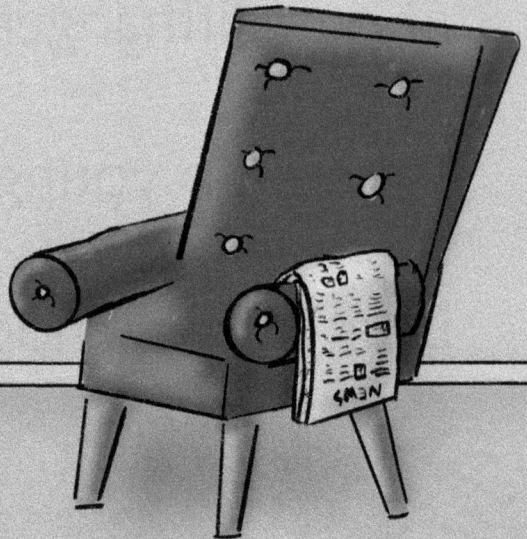

I have kleptomania, but when it gets bad, I take something for it.

My wife has begged me to stop making police related puns.
I said, "O.K......I'll give it arrest.

My Czech mate is surprisingly bad at chess.

Think I saw Michael J Fox earlier today in my local garden center.
Can't be certain though, as he had his back to the fuchsias.

What do ducks like on their tacos?
Quackamole.

I was feeling bad about the future,
but then I installed the new version
of Microsoft Office.
It improved my Outlook.

The invention of the wheel was
what got things rolling.

How do you make the
number one disappear?
You just add a
G and it's gone.

Shout out to my fingers. I can count on all of them.

Why did the dad joke
cross the road?
To get to the other sigh.

Why did the belt get arrested?
He held up a pair of pants.

What's wrong with dinosaur
morning breath?
Extincts.

What do you call a man who
stopped digging holes?
Douglas.

What is it called when a cat wins a dog show?
A CAT-HAS-TROPHY.

You'll always stay young if you live honestly, sleep sufficiently, work industriously, and lie about your age.

I knew I shouldn't steal
a mixer from work,
but it was a whisk
I was willing to take.

What did Delaware?
A New Jersey.

Job Interviewer: Where do you see
yourself in the next five years?
Me: I'd say my biggest weakness is
listening.

First rule of Thesaurus Club.
You don't talk, converse, discuss,
speak, chat, deliberate, confer,
gab, gossip or natter about
Thesaurus Club.

My Grandma always used to say,
"An apple a day keeps
the doctor away. "
I don't know if that's true,
or just one of
Granny's myths.

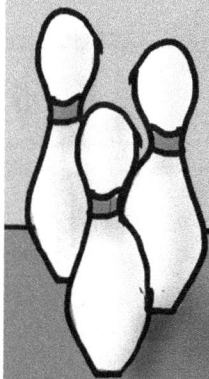

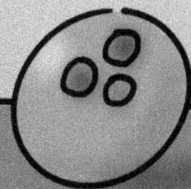

What kind of music should you
listen to while fishing?
Something catchy!

I told my wife that a husband
is like a fine wine: we just get
better with age.
The next day she locked me
in the cellar.

At the petting zoo, I saw a sheep
scratching itself.
Turns out it had fleece.

What did the sushi
say to the bee?
Wasabi.

What is better than getting straight A's in Pirate School?
Seven C's.

How many telemarketers does it take to change a light bulb?
Only one, but he has to do it during dinner.

A lot of people cry when they cut onions.
The trick is not to form an emotional bond.

How many apples grow on a tree?
All of them.

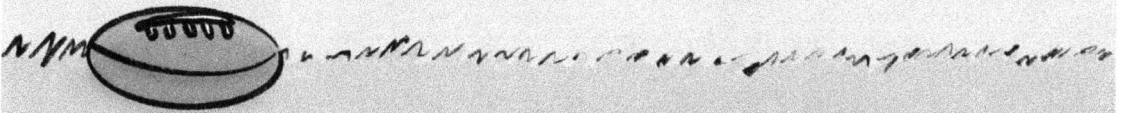

If you are impulsive, you should consider a career in dermatology. They are known for making rash decisions.

While at the grocery store, be careful not to knock over the cabbage display.
Heads will roll.

I asked my friend when their birthday was. He said March 1st. I stood up, walked around the room, and asked again.

What's the leading cause of dry skin?
Towels.

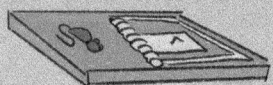

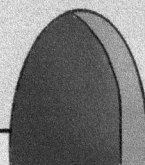

Why did alternate universe
Spider-Man do so well on
his driving test?
He was an excellent
Parallel Parker

Air used to be free at the gas
station, now it costs 2.50.
You want to know why?
Inflation.

Why did the chicken go
to the séance?
To get to the other side.

A woman in labor shouted,
"Shouldn't! Wouldn't! Didn't! Can't"
"Don't worry," said the doc.
"Those are just contractions."

Hear about the new restaurant
called Karma?
There's no menu:
You get what you deserve.

What does Charles Dickens
keep in his spice rack?
The best of thymes,
the worst of thymes.

Clones are people two.

What do you call a train carrying bubblegum?
A chew-chew train.

What type of sandals do frogs wear?
Open-toad.

You'll never be as lazy as whoever named the fireplace.

What musical instrument do you find in the bathroom?
A tuba toothpaste.

What's a forklift?
Food, usually.

What do you call a nervous javelin thrower?
Shakespeare.

Have you heard about
Competitive Camping?
It's in tents!

Tonight We are having Himalayan
rabbit stew for dinner.
We saw Himalayan on the side of
the road.

Want to hear a chimney joke?
I got stacks of them!
The first one is
on the house.

If I got 50 cents for every failed
math exam, I'd have $ 6.30 now.

I was going to make myself a belt
made out of watches, but then
I realized it would be a waist
of time.

I saw an ad for burial plots and
thought to myself this is the last
thing I need.

How much room should you give
fungi to grow?
As mushroom as possible.

My wife and I often laugh about
how competitive we are,
but I laugh more.

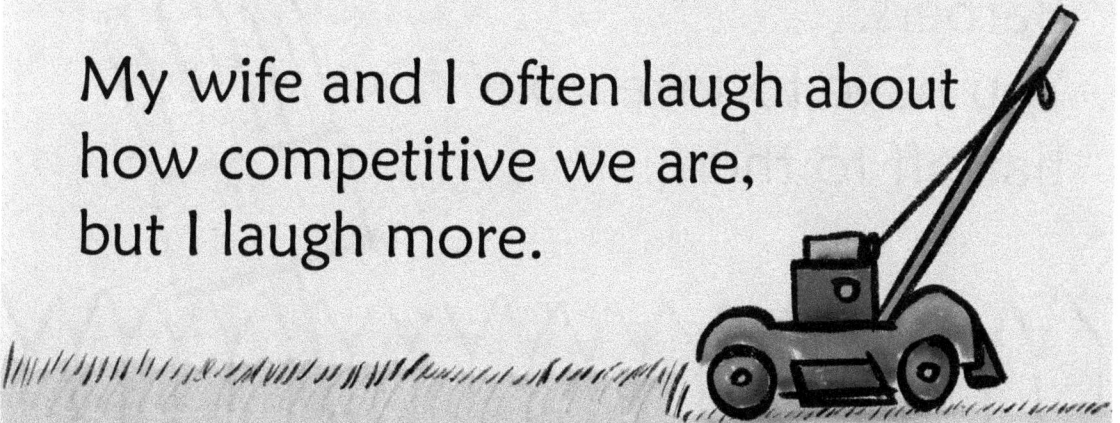

If you arrest a mime, do you have to
tell him he has the right to
remain silent?

Sometimes I use words I do not
understand so I can sound more
photosynthesis.

Reintarnation: When you come back
as a hillbilly.

Fired the janitor for smoking pot.
I can't stand high maintenance
people.

Barbers.
You have to take your
hat off to them.

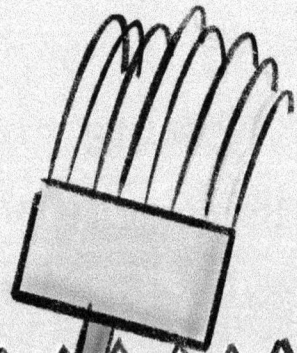

Advice to husbands:
Try praising your wife now and
then, even if it does startle
her at first.

What vegetable is cool,
but not that cool?
Radish.

If a plant is sad, do other
plants photosympathize with it?

The worst time to have a heart
attack is during a game
of charades.

Never take advice from electrons.
They are always negative.

When tempted to fight fire with fire,
always remember the fire
department usually uses water.

My wife told me to rub the herbs on
the meat for better flavor.
That's sage advice.

Waiter: How do you like your steak,
sir?
Sir: Like winning an argument with
my wife.
Waiter: Rare it is

What do you get when you cross
a fridge with a radio?
Cool Music

What do you call someone who is
afraid of Santa?
Clausterphobic.

Charles Dickens walks into a bar
and orders a Martini.
The bartender says,
"Olive or Twist?"

A history degree
is useless.
There's no
future in it.

What's red and moves up and
down?
A tomato in an elevator.

Where do math teachers go on
vacation?
Times Square

My wife found out I was cheating
after she saw all the letters
I was hiding...
She's never playing
Scrabble with
me again.

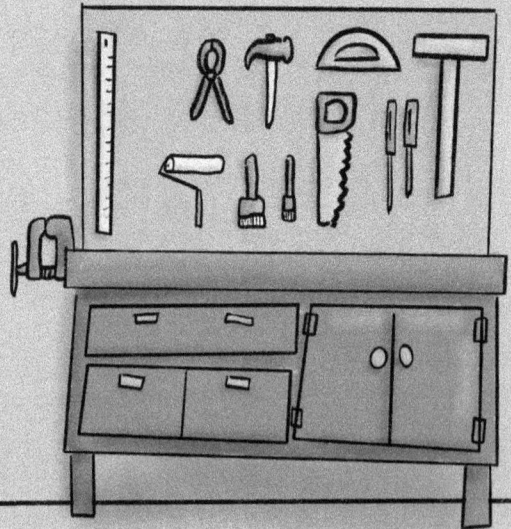

How does Moses make his coffee?
Hebrews it.

One harp says to another, "You're
too small to be a harp!"
The other says:
"What, you calling me a lyre?"

Why are piggy banks so wise?
They are filled with common cents.

Sorry sir, we do not serve time
travelers here.
A time traveler walks
into a bar.

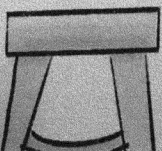

If you ride a bike twice in the same day, is that considered RECYCLING?

Why is Billy Joel's laundry still wet?
He did not start the dryer.

What do you use to cut a Roman Emperor's hair?
Ceasers.

How do you get a decent price on a sled?
You have toboggan.

Not knowing Greek mythology is my Achilles horse.

I taught my pet wolf how to meditate.
Now he is aware wolf.

I made some gumbo with only okra and sausage.
It was not bad and it was not good; it was just meaty okra.

Did you hear about the man who fell onto an upholstery machine?
He is now fully recovered.

If artists wear sketchers do linguists wear converse?

I was going sue U2 for stealing my songs, but my lawyer was pro-Bono.

Why did the chicken cross the mobius strip?
To get to the same side.

What do you call a laughing motorcycle?
A Yamahahaha

How many people who easily get distracted does it take to change a lightbulb?
Let's go ride bikes!

A giraffe walks into a bar.
"Sorry," says the bartender,
"We don't serve Heineken
here."

What do you call a knight
made entirely out of fine China?
Sir-amic

Why don't DJs make good
fisherman?
They are always dropping
the bass.

My favorite teacher back in
school was Mrs Turtle.
Funny name, but she
tortoise well.

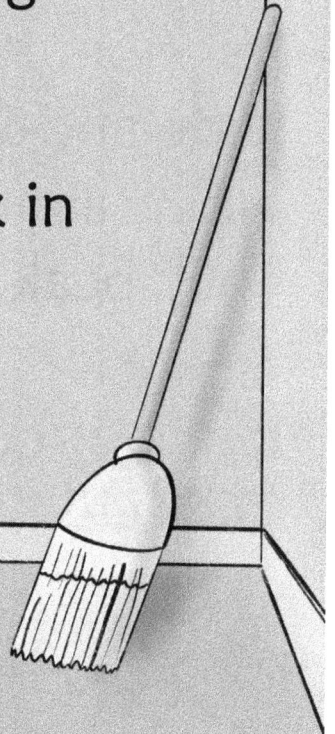

I went to a silent auction yesterday.
I got two dog whistles and a mime.

I asked the librarian where the books
on engine lubricants were.
She said they were in the
non-friction section.

I do not think it is fair that only
roosters are allowed to start the day
screaming.

It is pointless to play
Hide-and-Seek with
mountain ranges.
They peak.

Ice cream cone.
CONE!!!

CHAPTER 4:

ADVISOR
AMUSEMENTS

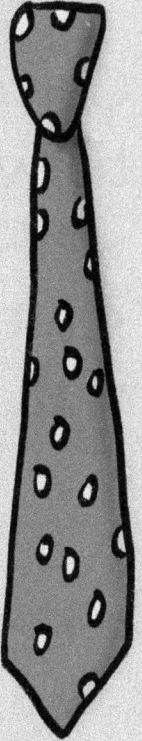

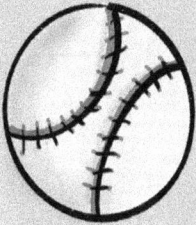

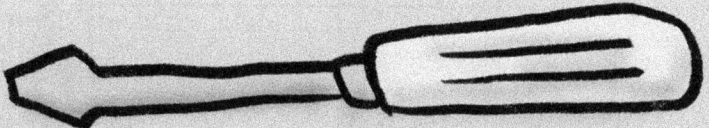

I went shopping at a cherry stand
and then a microphone store.
Bought a Bing. Bought a boom.

When I was young, we got a dog
and a cat.
The next day we named the dog
Curiosity.

Correct punctuation: the difference
between a sentence that's
well-written and a
sentence that's,
well, written.

A backwards poet
writes inverse.

Two parrots are sitting on a perch.
One turns to the other and asks,
"Do you smell fish?"

What is the difference between
ignorance and apathy?
I do not know, and I do not care.

On our way home my friend said:
"Let's stop and visit my brother
Nickolas".
So we took the see Nick route.

What do you call a clown in jail?
A silicon.

Local Area Network in Australia:
The LAN down under

Justice is best served cold.
If it was served warm, it would be justwater.

This morning I saw a guy dragging a clam on a leash.
And I thought, "It must be hard to walk with a pulled mussel".

I was a bookkeeper for 10 years.
The library was not too happy about it.

Lama spelled with one 'L' is a holy man. Llama with 2 Ls is a beast of burden. What is a three 'L' lama? A big fire in Boston.

I accidentally played 'dad' instead of 'dead' when the bear attacked. Now it can ride a bike without training wheels.

Yesterday I saw a guy spill all his Scrabble letters on the road.
I asked him,
"What's the word
on the street?"

Instead of naming my son Drew, I named him Driew.
It is only weird if you say it backwards.

I ate my last piece of cheese yesterday. Today it is raining.
Ain't no sunshine when cheese gone.

Why do dogs float in the water?
Because they are good buoys.

What did the femur say to the patella?
I kneed you.

"How much to buy a singing
ensemble?"
"Do you mean a choir?"
"Fine, how much to acquire
a singing ensemble?"

District:
The answer to the question,
"So, how strict are you going to be?"

I once bought a wooden car.
Wooden engine, wooden doors,
wooden wheels, wooden seats,
put the wooden key in
the wooden ignition.
Wooden start.

Where do crayons go on vacation?
Color-ado!

Who helps little pumpkins cross the
road on the way to school?
The Crossing Gourd.

We told the restaurant manager that
our salads were a bit on the dry side.
It was a situation that we felt needed
addressing.

How does Scooby travel by boat?
He "ruh-rows"

What should you do
if you are addicted
to seaweed?
Sea kelp.

My dog named Minton just ate a shuttlecock.
Bad Minton.

There is only one thing that scares me during Halloween.
My wife: "Which is?"
Me: "Exactly"

How do leaves get from place to place?
Autumn-mobiles.

I am not a huge fan of archery.
It has way too many drawbacks.

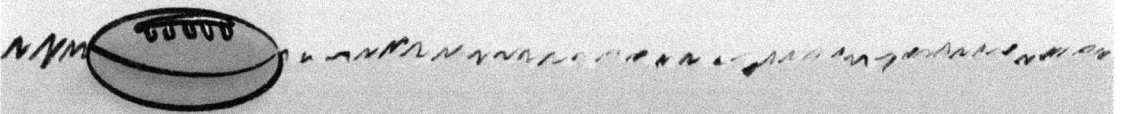

Induction: the act of inserting ducks.
Deduction: the act of removing ducks.

Did you know that trees are committed to one relationship at a time?
They practice mahogany.

My wife has accused me of stealing her Thesaurus.
Not only was I shocked, I was also aghast, appalled and dismayed.

I accidentally took my cat's meds last night..
Do not ask meow.

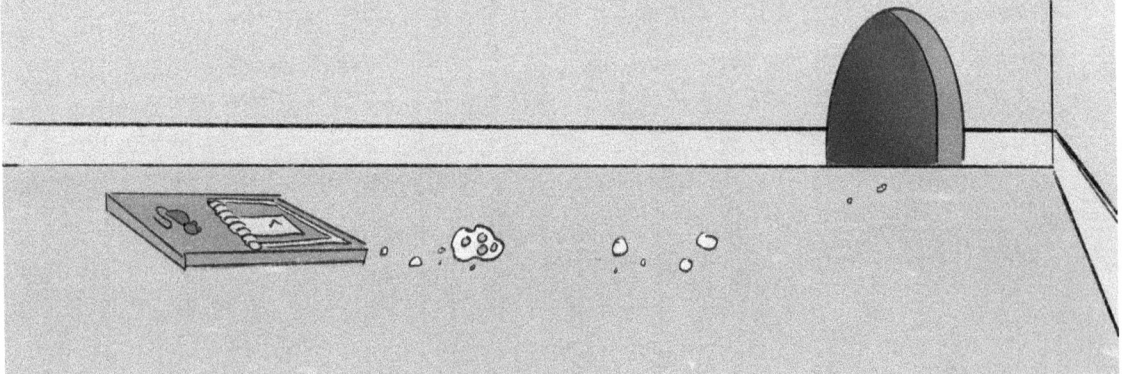

What do you call a French guy being
scratched by a cat?
Claude.

What do you do when
you see a space man?
Park your car, man.

If I ever run out of dad jokes
I've always got daylight savings time
puns to fall back on

How are false teeth like stars?
They come out at night

My kid refuses to eat fish. What do you think is a good replacement?
Cats. Cats love fish.

There's no "I" in denial.

I know a lot of you are sad because it's a Monday...
But don't forget, only 48 hours ago, it was a sadder day

What's the difference between Dubai and Abu Dhabi?
The people in Dubai don't like the Flintstones, but the people in Abu Dhabi do.

Where do bees go to the bathroom?
At the BP station.

The problem with kleptomaniacs is that they always take things literally.

My therapist says I have a preoccupation for revenge.
We'll see about that.

If a parsley farmer gets sued, can they garnish his wages?

My paper airplane will not fly.
That is because it is stationery.

Why do you never see elephants hiding in trees?
Because they're so good at it.

Why don't pirates take a bath before they walk the plank?
They just wash up on shore.

The bank keeps calling me to give me compliments.
They say I have an "outstanding balance."

Did you hear about the cat who ate a ball of yarn?
She had mittens.

I finally managed to convince my
wife to watch Back to the Future.
It's about time.

My friend called me for help,
claiming he had turned into a harp.
I raced over there only to find he
was a lyre.

I know a bunch of good jokes
about umbrellas, but they
usually go over
people's heads.

Why did dandelion
stop dating?
It kept getting
blown off.

What role do green beans play in
Thanksgiving dinner?
The casse-role.

I used to make loads of money
clearing leaves from gardens.
I was raking it in.

Did you hear about the surgeon
who enjoyed performing quick
surgeries on insects?
He did one on the fly.

Communism jokes aren't funny
unless everyone
gets them.

I'm an expert at picking leaves and
heating them in water.
It's my special tea.

My kids think I use outdated
technology.
But they're just ignoring the fax.

What's the difference between a cat
and a comma?
A cat has claws at the end of paws;
A comma is a pause at the
end of a clause.

I got into a fight with 1, 3, 5, 7 and 9.
The odds were against me.

So many people these days are too judgmental.
I can tell just by looking at them.

Did you hear about the apathetic rabbit?
He doesn't carrot all.

Did you hear you can buy carbon and iron for the price of just one alloy?
What a steel!

Drama:
A word boring people use to
describe fun people.

My granddad always said "When
one door closes another one opens"
Lovely man, but a terrible cabinet
maker.

Why do mushrooms get
invited to all the parties?
Because they are
such fungis.

The Improper Fraction
Helpdesk is now
open 24/7.

They are small hotels where guys
are reaching out to other very smart
guys.
In sum, in some inns, some men
summon some Mensa men.

It looks like I didn't get that job
at Microsoft.
They never responded
to my telegram.

Anything not related to elephants
is irrelephant.

Where are
mathematicians
buried?
The Symmetry.

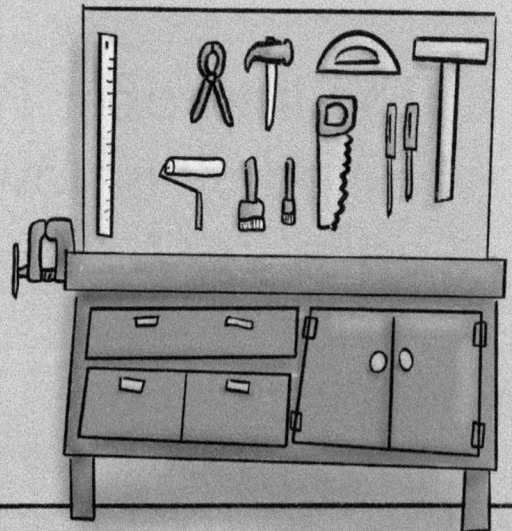

I know it's a long shot, but does anyone know what a Trebuchet is?

My wife thinks our kids are spoiled, but I believe most kids smell like that.

My wife said I have to stop making puns of world capitals.
You win some, Jerusalem.

The magazine about cardiovascular disease went out of business due to poor circulation.

Exercise? I thought you said extra fries.

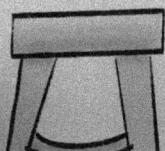

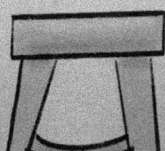

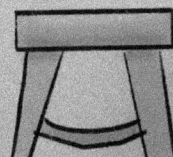

I HIGHLY RECOMMEND NOT
arguing with anyone at a buffet.
My goodness, they already have
enough on their plate.

I tried to build myself an armchair
but accidentally made it too wide.
So near, and yet sofa.

Did you hear the joke about the
lumberjack, the sheep and the goat?
I wood tell ewe, but it's baaaaaad.

What do you call a cow that just had
a baby?
Decaffeinated.

I was in a good mood till I started
petting a duckling in the park.
Then I started feeling a little down.

Last night I paused the movie to get
some snacks.
Now I've lost my job at the theater.

What New Year's resolution should a
basketball player never make?
To travel more .

What do you call a
scientist who snitches?
A lab rat.

I invented a new word!
Plagiarism!

Have you heard of the blind
cyclops brothers?
Neither have eye.

My teachers told me I'd never
amount to anything because I
procrastinate so much.
I told them, "Just you wait!"

Last night, my wife and I watched
three movies back-to-back.
Luckily, I was the one facing the TV.

What do you call nitrogen when
the sun comes up?
Daytrogen.

What is the digital camera's New Year's resolution?
1080p.

I got fired from the transmission factory, turns out I didn't put on enough shifts.

My neighbor is a veterinarian chiropractor.
He is an animal cracker.

I've been prescribed anti-gloating cream.
I can't wait to rub it in.

Volcanoes are earth pimples.

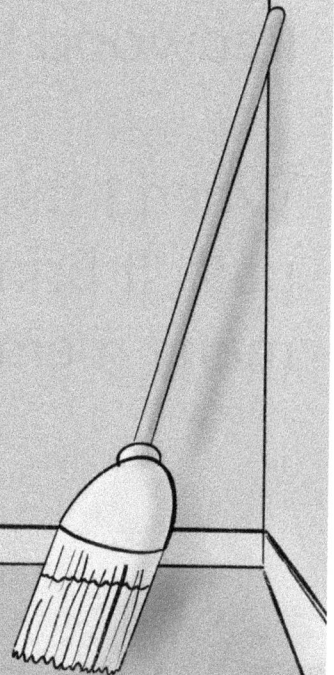

What do you call someone who takes care of chickens?
A chicken tender.

Why are green beans the most Zen of all vegetables?
Because they've found their inner peas.

After hours of research, I still can't make puns about trees.
You'd think everything I've Redwood help.

When I think about the past, it brings back so many memories.

Dentist: "You need a crown."
Patient: "Finally, someone who
understands me!"

Exaggerations have become an
epidemic.
They went up by a million percent
last year.

What did the Dorito farmer say to
the other Dorito farmer?
Cool Ranch!

I'm reading a book on
the history of glue.
I just can't seem
to put it down.

My balloon elephant wouldn't fit in the back seat of my car so I had to pop the trunk.

Man 1: I'm John Jacob Jingleheimer Schmidt, good sir. And you are?
Man 2: Buddy, you are not gonna believe this.

Never trust a train.
They have loco motives.

First week working at the bicycle factory and they already made me the spokes person.

CHAPTER 5

ELDER
EPIGRAMS

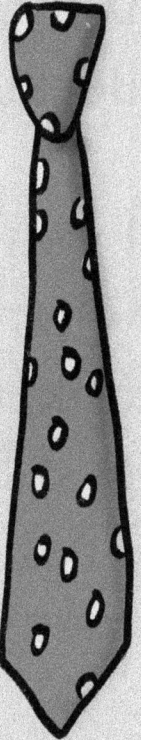

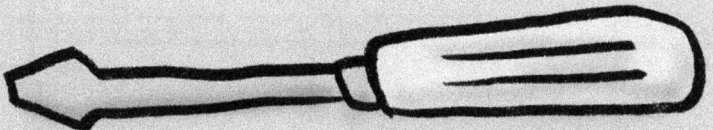

People appreciate when you go the extra mile, unless you are a taxi driver.

When i accidentally say something from Lord of the Rings in casual conversation that's a Frodoian Slip.

Why did the baker cross the road? Because he had muffin else to do.

I was walking down the street where the houses were numbered, 64k, 128k, 256k, 512k, and 1MB.
That was a trip down memory lane.

My Grandmother was 80% Irish.
Her name was Iris.

I have a fear of overly intricate
buildings.
I have a complex complex complex.

I'm great at solving labyrinths.
It only takes me a minotaur, too.

Tripped and hit my head on a
snare drum and now I think I
have a percussion.

My daughter wants to study
burrowing rodents.
I told her to gopher it.

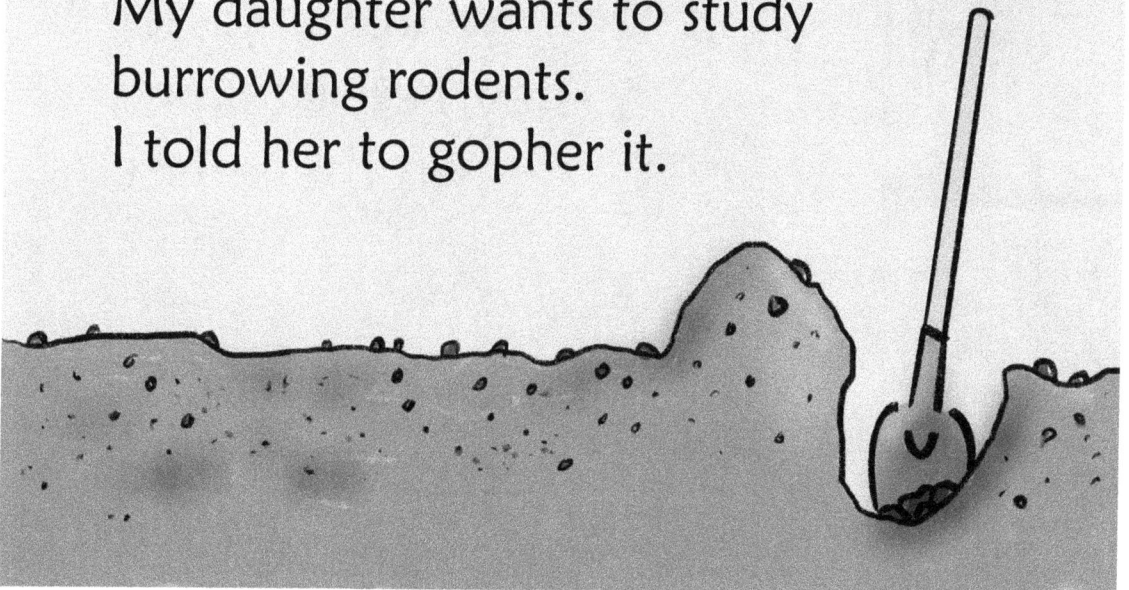

I don't always whoop.
But when I do, there it is.

I have a habit of taking pictures of
myself in the shower, but they
always come out too blurry.
I think I may have selfie steam
issues.

I was accused of being a plagiarist.
Their words, not mine.

How do you know if
Saturday and Sunday
love someone?
They get weekend
in the knees.

There are 10 different types of people in the world: Those who understand binary code and those who don't.

People are often surprised when they see the intricate tattoo that I got done in Madrid.
Nobody expects the Spanish ink precision.

I was thinking growing my hair long in the back and keeping it short in the front, but I probably ought to mullet over.

Why did the Easter egg hide?
Because he was a little chicken.

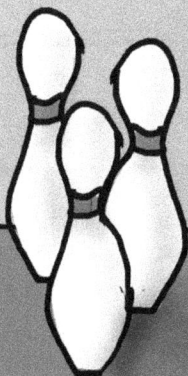

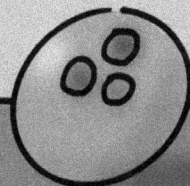

They're making a movie about
clocks.
It's about time.

My coworkers laugh at my jokes
at in-person meetings, but never in
online meetings.
When I asked them why, they said
that my jokes weren't remotely
funny.

I haven't seen my twin brother
since I left Australia.
We were separated
at Perth.

At a seafood restaurant I asked for a lobster tail.
The server smiled sweetly and said "Once upon a time, there was this handsome lobster…"

A king and queen walk into a bar. The bartender says, "Sorry, you're not 21."

What color is the wind?
Blew.

If your shirt is not tucked into your pants, then your pants are tucked into your shirt.

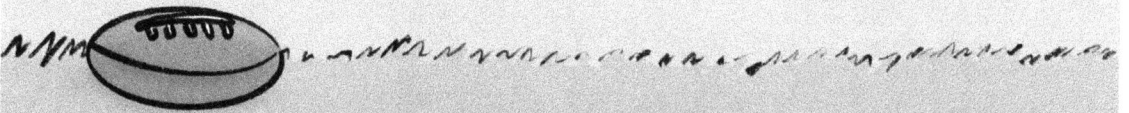

What's the definition of a will?
It's a dead giveaway.

I got thrown out of the Mime
meeting yesterday.
It must have been something I said.

I'm a really big fan of the
Bee Gees and I also like
cooking Chinese food.
You can tell by the way
I use my wok.

Did you hear the joke about the
bed?
I haven't made it yet.

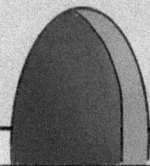

Did you know crocodiles could
grow up to 15 feet?
But most just have 4.

I decorated my living room with
some desks and a whiteboard.
It looks really classy.

I used to sneak out of my house
to go to parties.
Now I sneak out of parties to
go to my house.

What kind of cheese isn't yours?
Nacho cheese.

I've written a musical called 'Goldfish'
It's very similar to 'Cats',
although 'Memory' is a lot shorter.

In what key do cows sing?
Beef flat.

My credit card was declined at the sweater store, so the cashier had to ask for my cardigan.

INTERVIEWER: Can you explain this gap in your resume?
ODYSSEUS: Ok. It's actually a really long story.

The older I get, I regret all the people I've lost over the years. Being a trail guide wasn't such a great idea.

Had some mushrooms on toast this morning.
Breakfast of Champignons.

My wife and I can't agree on appropriate gardening footwear. But she's digging in her heels.

I really do regret buying the apartment above Lionel Richie.

Chris: Can I borrow a ten?
Kristen: Sure!
Christen: Thanks!
Kris: You're welcome!

Start a new job in Seoul next week.
I thought it would be a good Korea
move.

How do you make an egg-roll?
You push it.

Know what seems odd to me?
Numbers that aren't divisible by
two.

Why did the chicken click the PowerPoint presentation?
To get to the other slide.

What's it called when a gardener accidentally plants the wrong type of flower?
Oopsie daisy.

I told my wife to embrace her mistakes.
She gave me a hug.

I can tolerate algebra, maybe even a little calculus but geometry is where I draw the line.

What would bears be
without bees?
Ears.

What does corn say when it
gets a compliment?
Aw, shucks!

Where does a well-balanced
horse live?
A Stable.

What did the yoga instructor say
when her landlord tried
to evict her?
Namaste.

Would making nun's clothing be
considered habit forming?

Dear Naps,
I'm sorry I was a jerk to you when
I was a kid.

The Indian restaurant I work at is
so secretive I signed a legal
agreement I wouldn't share
the flatbread recipe
Just their standard naan
disclosure agreement.

We had a contest at work for the best neckwear...
It was a tie.

I can't believe I forgot to go to the gym today.
That's 7 years in a row now.

To the thief who took my anti-depressants...
I hope you are happy.

Keanu Reeves is not a big fan of April Fools.
He much more prefers the May tricks.

What did the French chef give his wife for Valentine's Day?
A hug and a quiche.

A cardiology video is totally clips of the heart.

What's the difference between a camera and a sock?
One takes photos, and the other takes five toes.

Running feels great unless you compare it to not running.

I don't believe in déjà vu and it feels like this isn't the first time I've said that.

Where do sheep go on vacation?
The Baaaahamas

What do you call a bagel that has mastered yoga?
A pretzel.

Think my local mechanic has amnesia. Took my car in for a new air filter and he asked me what year it was.

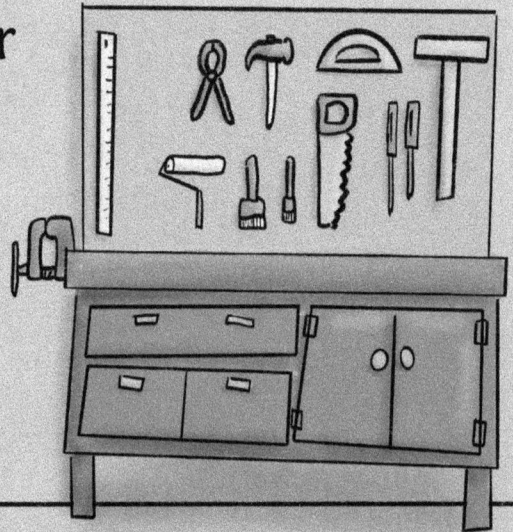

Everyone has been talking about your paranoia.

National Apathy Society:
Become a member or not.
We don't care.

I found stir fry all over my bed this morning.
I must've been sleep wokking again.

Some people always need their opinions validated.
Am I right ?

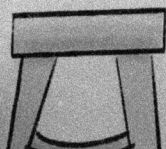

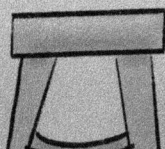

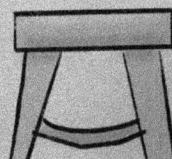

CHAPTER 6

HOLIDAY HUMOR

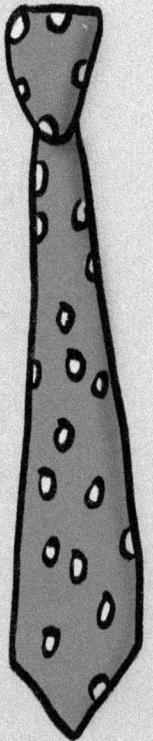

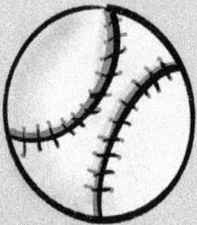

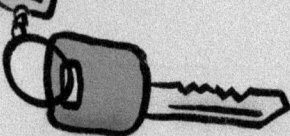

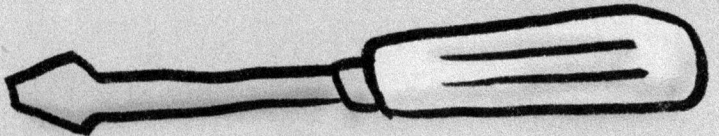

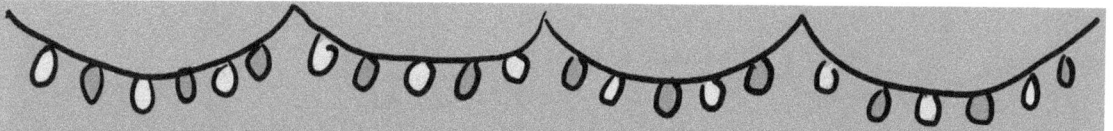

How did Scrooge win the football game?
The ghost of Christmas passed.

What do you call Santa when he stops moving?
Santa Pause.

My biggest fear is being trapped in a small room with Santa.
I have Claustrophobia.

The Christmas alphabet is almost identical to the standard English alphabet except that it has Noel.

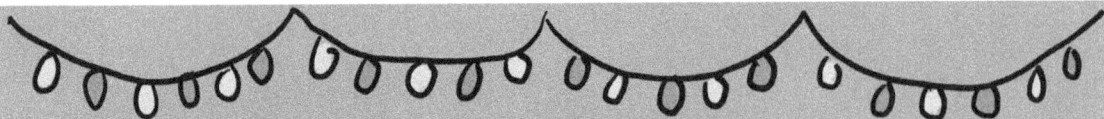

What do you call Santa's helpers?
Subordinate Clauses.

What do Santa's elves listen to
whilst they work?
Wrap music.

What do you call a cat sitting on
the beach on Christmas Eve?
Sandy Claws

Why will Santa go down your
chimney on Christmas Eve?
Because it soots him.

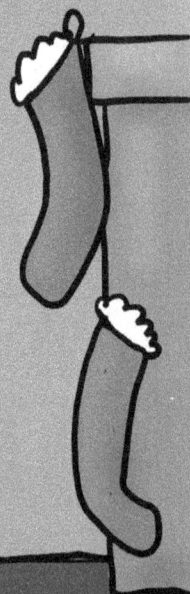

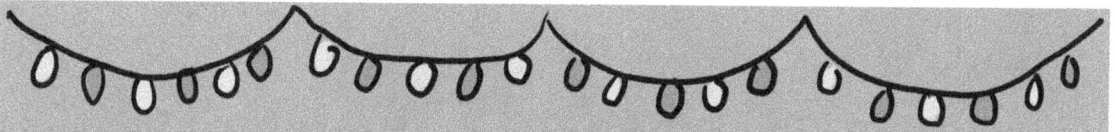

I have bought my wife a fridge
for Christmas.
I can't wait to see her face light
up when she opens it.

Why was Santa sick on the
day after Christmas?
A couple of the chimneys
he went down had the flue.

Why was Santa's little helper
depressed?
He had low elf-esteem.

What goes "Oh Oh Oh"?
Santa walking
backwards.

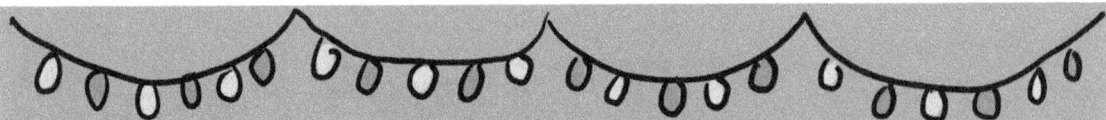

I bought my wife the biography
of a famous British explorer in the
South Pacific.
She said she wanted a Cook book
for Christmas.

How did the ornament get
addicted to Christmas?
He was hooked on trees his
whole life!

What's the difference between
the Christmas alphabet and
the regular alphabet?
The Christmas alphabet
has noel.

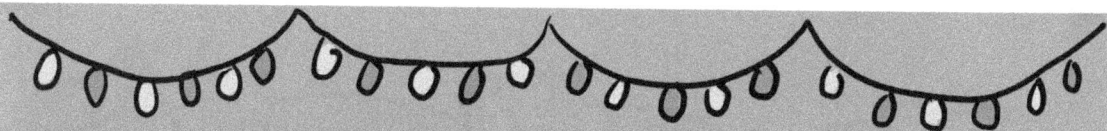

Did you hear that Santa knows karate?
He has a black belt.
What is Santa's primary language?
North Polish.

How does Santa remember all the fireplaces he's visited?
He keeps a log.

Christmas!
The time when everyone gets santamental.

How do Christmas trees get ready for a party?
They spruce up!

BONUS SECTION

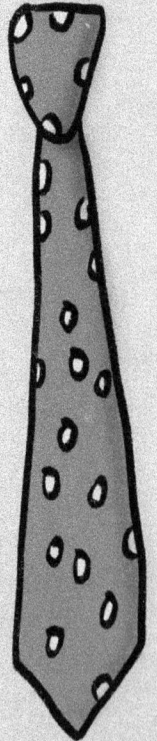

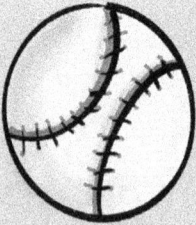

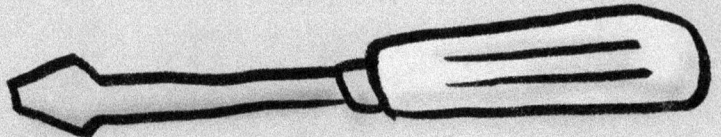

When we were preparing to launch the sequal 'Dadder Jokes' we ran a crowdfunding campaign that offered some unique perks, including variant covers designed by incredibly talented artists.

The creativity and skill that went into these alternate covers were so remarkable that we felt it would be a shame not to share them with all of our readers. So, in this sequel book, we've included a showcase of these stunning pieces of cover design art that were done for 'Dadder Jokes'.

We hope you enjoy this behind-the-scenes look at some alternative covers gracing your copy of this book.

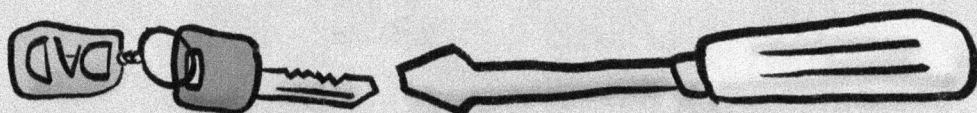

DADDER JOKES

CORNY AND CLEAN!

OVER 500 MORE GROANS & CHUCKLES!

MARK GONYEYA

BRYAN BALLINGER

DAD
JOKES
COVERS

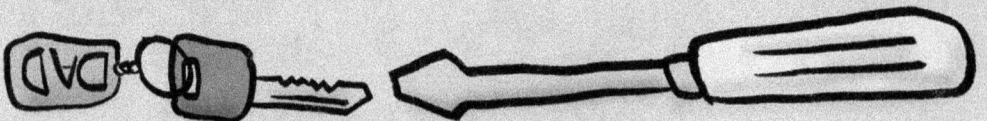

ORIGINAL COVER

PUBLISHED COVER

DAD JOKES

CORNY AND CLEAN!

OVER 500 GROANS & CHUCKLES

MARK GONYEYA

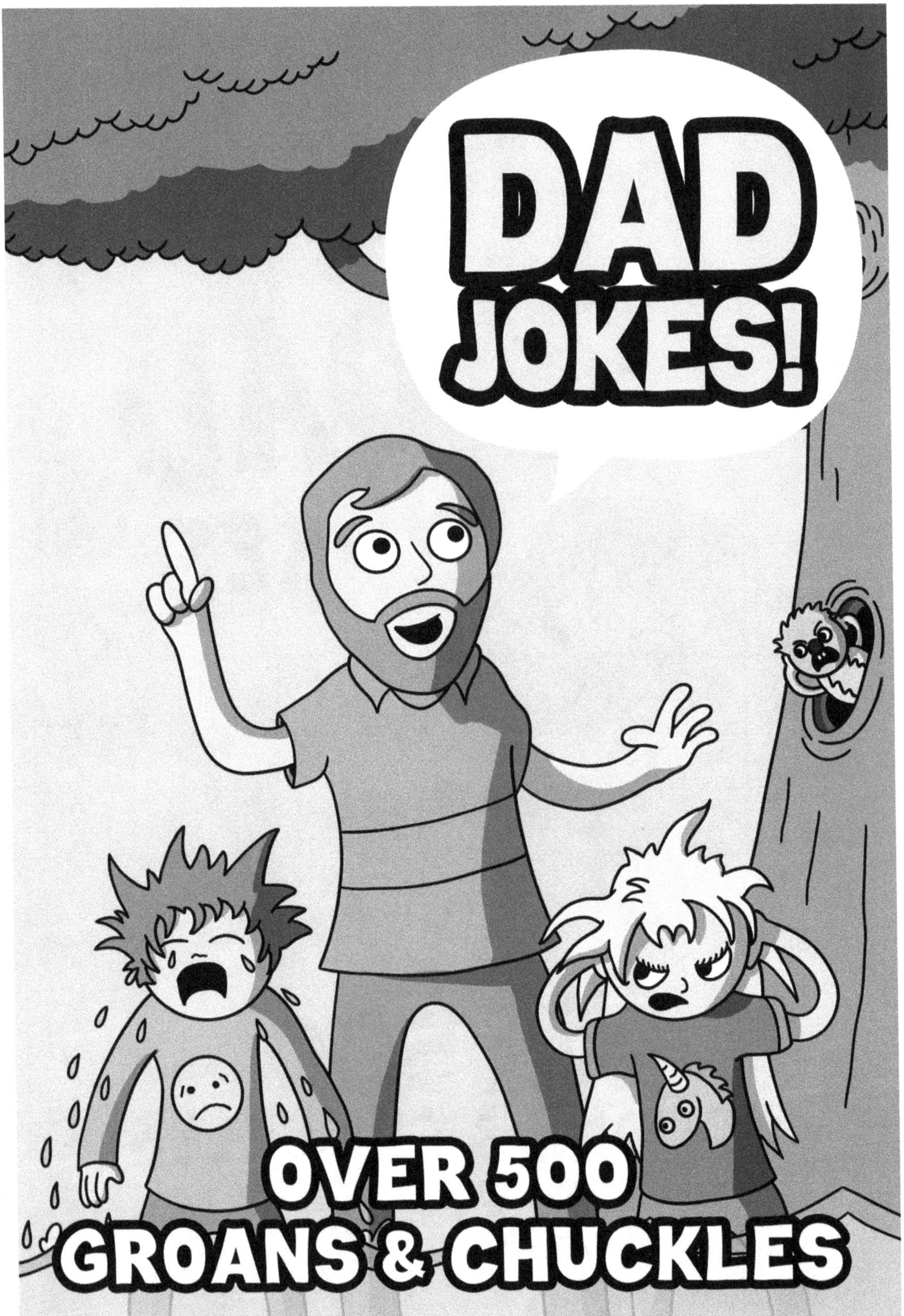

DIRK STANLEY

THANK YOU TO OUR KICKSTARTER BACKERS!

ABBY A

AMY KUKTA

AUTHOR DA TROTTER

BENJAMIN HIGGINS

BRAD VIETJE

CATCH DA CRAZE PODCAST

DALE COOPER

DALE WILSON

YODA FROM BANI KOUBEYE NIGER

DISMAY COMICS

DOUG SHUTE

HEATHER FARRINGTON

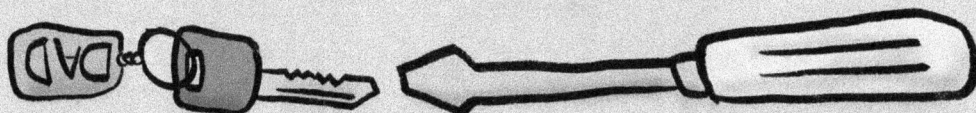

THANK YOU TO OUR KICKSTARTER BACKERS!

James "FAQs" Boyce
Hexetoes
Jay Lichtenauer
John Henry Muhrer
Jorge "get your Medz" Medina
Kath Towers
Kristian Horn
Guido
Laurie "Total Descruction" Calcaterra
Marek
Mark G
Matt Forsyth

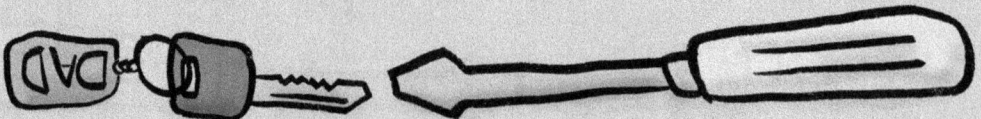

Thank You to our Kickstarter Backers!

PLUGOARTS

Peter McQuillan

Two Dimension Podcast

Sarah Swanson

Simian Circle Games

S Pitsirilos

Ten Schippnick

The Creative Fund by BackerKit

Traversing the Stars

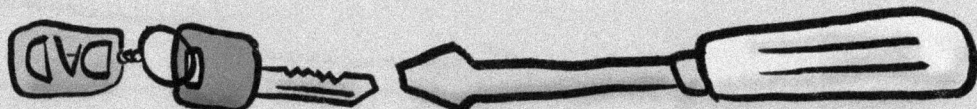

KEEP LAUGHING AT CORNY JOKES AND PUNS.
SEE YOU IN OUR THIRD INSTALLMENT:

DADDEST JOKES

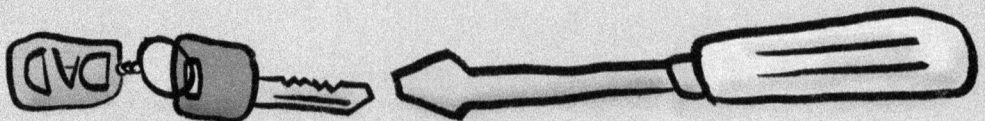

I TOLD MY CARPENTER I DIDN'T WANT CARPETED STEPS.
HE GAVE ME A BLANK STAIR.

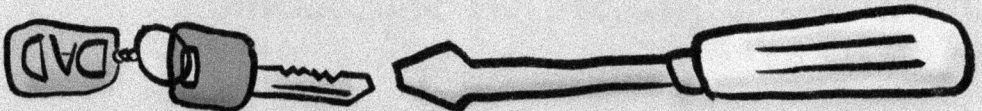

ABOUT THE AUTHOR

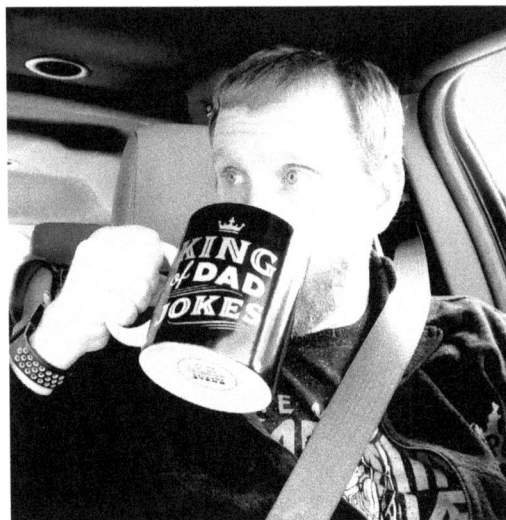

BARNEY SMITH:
WRITER, ILLUSTRATOR, ADVENTURER.
CAPTURING THE ESSENCE OF DAD JOKES
AND INTERCULTURAL MARRIAGE IN SATIRICAL
GRAPHIC NOVELS. FOUNDER OF
STORYCOMIC.COM, A GLOBAL PLATFORM
CELEBRATING DIVERSE NARRATIVES.
INSPIRING MINDS THROUGH ART,
STORYTELLING, AND BOUNDLESS CURIOSITY.

LEARN MORE AT: STORYCOMIC.COM

www.ingramcontent.com/pod-product-compliance
Lightning Source LLC
Chambersburg PA
CBHW081250040426

42452CB00015B/2768